INVESTIGATING NATURAL DISASTERS

INVESTIGATING
FLOODS

BY ELIZABETH ELKINS

raintree

D0258814

Raintree is an imprint of Capstone Global Library Limited, a company incorporated in England and Wales having its registered office at 264 Banbury Road, Oxford, OX2 7DY – Registered company number: 6695582

www.raintree.co.uk
myorders@raintree.co.uk

Edited by Alesha Sullivan
Designed by Steve Mead
Picture research by Morgan Walters
Production by Laura Manthe
Printed and bound in India.

ISBN 978 1 4747 3515 5 (hardback)
21 20 19 18 17
10 9 8 7 6 5 4 3 2 1

ISBN 978 1 4747 3519 3 (paperback)
22 21 20 19 18
10 9 8 7 6 5 4 3 2 1

British Library Cataloguing in Publication Data
A full catalogue record for this book is available from the British Library.

Photo Credits
Capstone Press, 11, 13; Getty Images: Barbara Zanon, 15, Bloomberg, 27; Shutterstock: Danny E Hooks, 12, dcwcreations, middle 29, goir, bottom 29, guentermanaus, 8, ikonacolor, (water vector) Cover, John Williams RUS, (wood texture) Cover, Markus Gebauer, 16, MaxyM, Cover, Nathan Holland, 18, 19, Nik Merkulov, design element throughout, cover, Phil MacD Photography, 5, Ruud Morijn Photographer, 10, Sergey Zaykov, 6 , 7, thomas koch, 20, Vadym Zaitsev, 25, VladimirCeresnak, design element, Volodymyr Krasyuk, top 29, Yanfei Sun, 22

CONTENTS

WATER, WATER
EVERYWHERE
4

FLOOD BASICS
6

WHERE DO
FLOODS
HAPPEN? 10

AFTERMATH
16

THE WORST
FLOODS IN THE
WORLD 18

A CHANGING
CLIMATE 24

MANAGING
FLOODS 26

STAYING
SAFE 28

GLOSSARY
30

READ MORE
31

WEBSITES
31

COMPREHENSION
QUESTIONS
32

INDEX
32

WATER, WATER EVERYWHERE

It was December 2015. Heavy rainfalls soaked England, Scotland, Ireland and Wales. One area received 36.3 centimetres (14.3 inches) of rain in only 24 hours. Thousands of homes were flooded. Bridges were damaged, and in many places travel was disrupted. People fled their homes with the help of the military and lifeboat services.

Defenses, such as sandbags and **barriers**, were put in place to help stop flooding in Cumbria. But the sandbags and barriers did not keep the water away from homes and businesses. More storms followed all month. The flooding grew even worse as rivers overflowed their banks. More than 20,000 homes across the United Kingdom were left without electricity.

EL NIÑO

Heavy rainfall in the winter is unusual. These rains were partly due to a weather pattern called **El Niño**. This climate cycle raises ocean water temperatures and brings large amounts of rain to different parts of the world. El Niño weather patterns do not happen regularly. They usually occur every two to seven years.

The British Army helped rescue people trapped in their homes from the flooding in the UK in 2015.

barrier gate used to control the flow of a body of water

El Niño complex series of climatic changes affecting the equatorial Pacific region and beyond every few years

FLOOD BASICS

Floods are the most common natural disasters in the world. They threaten lives and property. They cause damage that takes years to fix. And many times people are powerless to stop them.

A flood happens when the ground isn't able to soak up water. The water rises until it is a few centimetres deep and sometimes many metres deep. Water may arrive suddenly or creep slowly higher. Sometimes the water drains away quickly. Other times an area stays flooded for weeks.

Not every flood is the same. Overbank flooding happens when water from melting snow or a heavy rain overflows the banks of a river. The water creeps up across nearby land. Flash floods send fast-moving water through an area and are very dangerous. These floods happen so fast that there is very little warning. They can be caused by large amounts of rain falling in a short amount of time. This makes fast-moving water rise very quickly. Floods can also be caused by a dam bursting or **levee** failing, sending a huge volume of water downstream in an instant.

Heavy rain in a short period of time can cause dangerous flash flooding.

levee bank built up near a river to prevent flooding

Ice jam floods happen in winter when ice forms. Heavy rain pushes chunks of river ice together. They form a dam. Water piles up behind the ice and spills onto nearby land. When the ice breaks up or melts a large amount of water is suddenly released. This causes floods downstream.

FACT

Floods can also happen when a volcano erupts. Lahar, which is a thick mixture of water and debris, can clog rivers and cause flooding.

A landslide caused by heavy rains destroyed a street in Amazonas, Brazil, in 2008.

Mud from landslides can also cause flooding. Debris from landslides can be carried by water as it flows down a slope. It can pick up trees and the remains of building and bridges. When the material reaches a river, it creates a dam that holds back the water and causes flooding.

Floods can also happen because of big storms. Hurricane Sandy, in 2012, brought so much rain to the New York City, USA, area that large parts of the city were flooded. The subway tunnels and coastal parts of the city were under water.

CAUSES OF FLOODS

▶ Melting snow causes a river to rise steadily. The water overflows its banks, creeping into nearby fields and homes.

▶ Heavy rainfall makes a river rise quickly, sending a surge of water pouring down a hillside.

▶ A dam breaks and releases the water it had been holding.

▶ A hurricane or strong storm pushes water onto the coast.

▶ A large amount of rain falls onto dry, hard soil and cannot be absorbed.

▶ Heavy rainfall brings more water than a city's sewer system can carry away. The flood fills city streets, and water may flow into people's gardens and homes.

WHERE DO FLOODS HAPPEN?

Floods can occur almost anywhere. **Floodplains** are important. They provide a place for water to go when snow melts or heavy rain falls. This water helps carry nutrients to the floodplain's soil. The nutrients make it easier for plants to grow. Floods can also help control **erosion**. When floodwaters spread over a large area, the water flows slower than it would if it was in a narrow riverbed. Less soil is worn away from riverbanks when water moves slowly.

A floodplain is generally a flat area of land near a stream or river.

Floods can affect buildings constructed on floodplains. These are the areas around rivers where water overflows during a flood. The area closest to the river is called the floodway. The water here will probably be flowing when a flood occurs. The area at the edge of the floodplain is called the floodway fringe. The fringe area might have standing water during a flood. Floodplains are a natural way to handle excess water. But when people build homes too close to a floodplain, the homes are at risk of flooding.

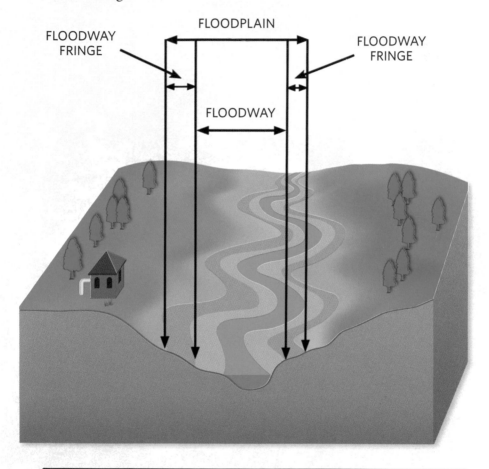

floodplain area of low land near a stream or river that becomes flooded during heavy rains

erosion wearing away of land by water or wind

Areas that receive heavy rainfall experience more flooding. The country of Bangladesh in South Asia receives heavy rainfall during the **monsoon** season. This is the most flood-prone area in the world. On the other hand, places that are usually dry, such as deserts or regions that do not receive regular rainfall, often flood because of storms. If the ground is very dry and hard, rainwater cannot soak in. Instead rain runs across the surface and can cause flash floods.

FLOODS AND WILDLIFE

Flooded areas are important resting places for animals. Birds flying north or south stop in flooded fields and wetlands to eat. In 2010 an oil spill in the Gulf of Mexico endangered many birds that lived in the marshes off the coast. Farmers in Louisiana, USA, were asked to purposely flood fields so birds would have places to rest and find food.

Places that get a lot of snow in the winter may have floods when the snow melts in the spring. Melting snow causes river levels to rise. Spring rains also bring more water to rivers and may cause riverbanks to overflow.

Some coastal cities may be affected by hurricanes. These storms bring heavy rains and can cause a storm surge. This happens when winds push water towards the shore. A storm surge creates higher sea levels, which move inland and cause flooding.

FACT

New York City may see sea levels rise as much as 1.8 metres (6 feet) over the next 75 years. Many parts of the city could one day be under water.

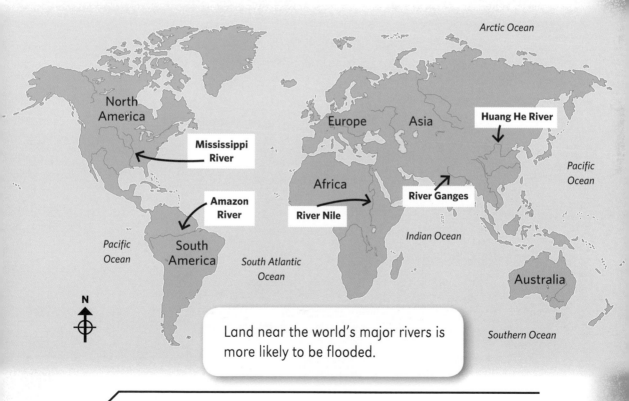

Land near the world's major rivers is more likely to be flooded.

monsoon very strong seasonal wind that brings heavy rains and hot, dry weather

Some cities that are in danger of flooding have built a system of huge gates that can be raised and lowered when high water threatens the area. London, England, and Venice, Italy, are two cities where high water levels often create flooding. London built gates on the River Thames called the Thames Barrier. The gates can be raised and lowered when the river's level rises. This controls the amount of water flowing into nearby rivers. Venice is in the building stages of constructing MOSE, which stands for Modulo Sperimentale Elettromeccanico. MOSE is a system of flap gates that will raise and lower where the city's **lagoon** meets the sea. The gates will hold back the high tides that bring floodwater into the city's canals.

Researchers are also working on a high-tech system that uses environmental data from **satellites**, weather balloons and computer models to predict flood risks. Satellite images show forecasters where clouds and heavy rain may be present. Weather balloons carry instruments that measure wind speed, air pressure and temperature. Computer simulations use information on wind speed and air pressure to create models. The models show which areas may experience storms in the days ahead. The data collected from this technology can help predict storms and floods. Giving people early warning about floods will provide more time for evacuation and may prevent flood-related deaths.

The MOSE project in Italy is intended to protect Venice from high waters and flooding.

FACT

The city of Venice experiences *acqua alta*, meaning high water, often in the winter. It is a very high tide that floods the city's canals, squares and walkways.

lagoon shallow pool of seawater separated from the sea by a narrow strip of land

satellite spacecraft that circles Earth; satellites gather and send information

AFTERMATH

The damage from floods can be extensive and long-lasting. Floods can be deadly. Thousands of people around the world die in floods each year. Floods can also leave behind extensive damage. Buildings and cars are often washed away. Vehicles that have been covered in water are often too damaged to repair. Roads are destroyed, and pavements buckle and crack. Bridges may be swept away. If floodwater covers farm fields, crops are often spoiled.

A house stands alone in a flooded area in Australia in 2011.

FACT

By the year 2050, flood damage in Europe is expected to cost £24 billion a year, mostly due to climate change and coastal city flooding.

Homes that are still standing after a flood may be permanently damaged. Floodwaters can soak mattresses and furniture. Carpets and floors may be wet or coated with mud. The flood may have carried **sewage** into the house. The home's **foundation** could be ruined, making the home unsafe. Even after clean-up, mould may grow in walls and insulation and make people sick.

When a dam holding back iron-mining waste burst in Mariana, Brazil, in 2015, a flood of thick, red, toxic mud smothered the town. The flood flattened buildings and trees and killed people and animals. Drinking water was polluted, and rivers were filled with red **sludge**. Wildlife was killed. It will take a very long time for the environment to recover.

sewage liquid and solid waste that is carried away in sewers and drains

foundation solid structure on which a building is built

sludge wet, muddy mixture

THE WORST FLOODS IN THE WORLD

One of the worst floods in the United States took place on 31 May 1889, in Johnstown, Pennsylvania. A dam on the Little Conemaugh River broke, sending 18 million metric tons of water moving at 64 kilometres (40 miles) per hour. It rushed 23 kilometres (14 miles) downhill into Johnstown with no warning. More than 2,200 people died, and some of their bodies were never found. Property damages reached more than £13 million.

Hurricane Katrina hit the US city of New Orleans, Louisiana, on 28 August 2005. The storm caused massive flooding when the levees that held back the waters of Lake Pontchartrain were damaged or swept away. Floodwaters poured into the city. In some areas people had to scramble into attics and onto rooftops to escape the rising water. More than 80 per cent of the city was under water. Almost 2,000 people died, and there was more than £76 billion in damage.

Flooding caused by Hurricane Katrina was one of the United States' most expensive natural disasters in history.

The flooding in Pakistan in 2010 destroyed thousands of people's homes and businesses.

The Indus River in Pakistan flooded in 2010. The monsoon rains there had released a record amount of rainfall. Some parts of the country in the northern mountains experienced flash floods. These floodwaters then moved downriver, sweeping away roads and bridges. Large areas of farmland were under water. The contaminated floodwaters made drinking water unsafe and destroyed food crops. More than 2,000 people died, and millions more suffered from homelessness, disease and starvation.

The United Kingdom suffered severe flooding in 2012. In North Wales the River Elwy rose to 4.3 metres (14 feet), which is twice its usual level. An elderly woman drowned when she was unable to get out of her house as it filled with water. Volunteers worked day and night using boats to ferry people from their homes to dry ground. People trapped on an island had to be rescued by aircraft. Over 500 homes were evacuated. Even with these valiant efforts, five people died.

Flooding in 2009 caused by the high river level of the Huang He in South China destroyed homes and businesses.

In 2004 Indonesia suffered widespread flooding from a tsunami after an earthquake struck. A tsunami is a huge wave or series of waves caused by the movement of the ocean floor from an earthquake. Waves more than 30 metres (100 feet) high brought massive amounts of water onto the land. Trees and buildings were flattened. People were swept away and drowned. Witnesses say the waves sounded like a freight train. Huge tsunami waves hit coastal areas all around the Indian Ocean, killing more than 230,000 people in 14 countries. It was the worst flooding disaster in recent history.

The Huang He River in China has flooded many times in the last 150 years. Researchers estimate a total of 7 million people have died from the Huang He flooding or from food shortages when crops have been destroyed. The Huang He usually floods because **silt** is deposited in the riverbed. The silt raises the river level until the water overflows its banks. Thousands of miles surrounding the river are then covered in water. Many dams have been built to help control the flooding.

FACT

The 2004 tsunami in Indonesia killed many people but spared others. A lucky baby was found floating in the floodwaters on a mattress, alive and well.

silt small particles of soil that settle at the bottom of a river, lake or ocean

A CHANGING CLIMATE

Flooding is expected to happen more frequently in the future because of climate change. The amount of rain that falls during the heaviest downpours is increasing as the average temperature is increasing in some regions. This is because warmer air holds more moisture than colder air. If the temperatures around the world continue to increase, scientists predict that rainfall may also increase by as much as 40 per cent. More rainfall will mean more flooding. Higher sea levels will also bring more flooding to coastal areas.

Humans often make choices that increase the chances of their homes flooding. People are building homes and other structures on floodplains, so when rivers rise, the chances of flooding are greater. People are also paving over more of the landscape for roads and car parks. Paved surfaces do not absorb water. When there is a heavy downpour, the water has to flow to unpaved areas, which can cause flooding.

FACT

Climate change is also causing bigger blizzards. This simply means that heavy precipitation is falling as snow in the winter instead of as rain in warmer weather.

Climate change may bring increased precipitation to many parts of the globe.

MANAGING FLOODS

It might seem that there is very little that can be done to avoid flooding. But experts are working to reduce floods and the damage they cause. Scientists in Japan have designed a system of huge underground tanks. Rainwater from rivers and **channels** flows into these tanks. Then the water is safely pumped into other rivers that are located away from the centre of cities. The huge pumps can release the equivalent of a swimming pool's worth of water every second.

PREVENTATIVE MEASURES

Some engineering practices can help prevent floods from getting out of control. Car parks paved with a special type of concrete that water can seep through are less likely to flood. Rain gardens are dips in the land, planted with shrubs, flowers and bushes. When water fills the dip, it holds the water as the plants soak up the excess through their roots. A balancing lake, also called a flood pond, is a dry area meant to contain extra water during a storm. These ponds are usually located next to rivers, streams and lakes.

channel narrow stretch of water between two areas of land

The Metropolitan Area Outer Underground Discharge Channel, an underground tank, in Kasukabe City, Japan, helps protect the city against flooding.

Another important tool experts use to manage floods is a river gauge. Gauges measure the depth of rivers and how fast water is flowing. A river gauge records data every 15 to 60 minutes. The data lets weather forecasters know which rivers are at, or near, flood stage. The forecasters can then warn people to get out of an area before a flood becomes dangerous.

STAYING SAFE

There are many things you can do to make sure you and your family stay safe during flooding. Here is a helpful list of dos and don'ts:

✓ DO:

Listen to local weather and emergency broadcasts. They will issue flood warnings that tell you to evacuate to higher ground.

If a flood happens, move to higher ground and stay away from flooded areas.

If you can't get out of your house, move to the top floor, attic or roof.

Keep a battery-powered radio on hand to listen to news reports and alerts.

If you are travelling, avoid places that might flood, such as valleys or floodplains.

✗ DON'T:

Do not drive into flooded areas. Roads may have collapsed, the water might be deeper than it looks, or your car could be swept away.

Do not wade into a flowing stream that reaches past your ankles. Even flowing water beneath knee-level can knock you off your feet.

Do not swim or play in floodwater. It may be contaminated.

Do not camp near rivers or streams.

Do not touch any electrical equipment if you are standing in water.

FLOOD EMERGENCY KIT

It is a good idea to make an emergency kit for bad weather. It will help you be prepared in any disaster. It should include:

- **a battery-powered torch or lantern**

- **a battery-powered radio**

- **extra batteries**

- **drinking water**

- **food that will not go bad, such as tinned goods (don't forget the tin opener) or boxed snacks**

- **first aid supplies**

FIRST AID KIT

GLOSSARY

barrier gate used to control the flow of a body of water

channel narrow stretch of water between two areas of land

El Niño complex series of climatic changes affecting the equatorial Pacific region and beyond every few years

erosion wearing away of land by water or wind

floodplain area of low land near a stream or river that becomes flooded during heavy rains

foundation solid structure on which a building is built

lagoon shallow pool of seawater separated from the sea by a narrow strip of land

levee bank built up near a river to prevent flooding

monsoon very strong seasonal wind that brings heavy rains and hot, dry weather

satellite spacecraft that circles Earth; satellites gather and send information

sewage liquid and solid waste that is carried away in sewers and drains

silt small particles of soil that settle at the bottom of a river, lake or ocean

sludge wet, muddy mixture

READ MORE

Fierce Floods (Planet in Peril), Cath Senker (Wayland, 2014)

The World's Worst Floods (World's Worst Natural Disasters), John R. Baker (Raintree, 2016)

Tsunamis (Nature Unleashed), Louise and Richard Spilsbury (Franklin Watts, 2017)

WEBSITES

flood-warning-information.service.gov.uk
View flood warnings currently issued for England and Wales on the Flood Information Service website.

news.bbc.co.uk/cbbcnews/hi/newsid_1610000/ newsid_1613800/1613858.stm
Read about what floods are and why they happen on the CBBC Newsround website.

www.ngkids.co.uk/science-and-nature/causes-of-floods
Find out more about the causes of floods, and read about children's experiences, on the National Geographic website.

COMPREHENSION QUESTIONS

1. Why can large amounts of rain actually be dangerous in a very dry place?

2. What are some things that humans are doing that can cause floods and increase flood damage?

3. What are some things that you and your family can do to prepare for a flood?

INDEX

Bangladesh 12
Brazil 17

causes of floods 6–7, 8–9, 12–13
China 23
climate change 24

El Niño 4

flood damage 4, 16–17, 8–19, 21, 23
floodplains 10–11, 24
floodway fringe 11
floodways 11

Hurricane Katrina 19
Hurricane Sandy 9

Indonesia 23
Italy 14
    Modulo Sperimentale Elettromeccanico (MOSE) 14

Japan 26

landslides 9

military 4

Pakistan 21

researching floods
    computer models 14
    satellites 14
    weather balloons 14

sandbags 4
staying safe 28–29

Thames Barrier 14
tsunamis 23
types of floods
    flash floods 7, 12, 21
    ice jam floods 8
    overbank floods 7, 13, 23
    storm surges 13

United Kingdom 4, 14, 21
United States 9, 12, 18–19